D1639599

Resource Centre
Diocesan Office
Old Alresford Place
Alresford SO24 9DH
01962 737349

Walking in the light

100 prayers for children

David Adam

**kevin
mayhew**

First published in 2008 by

KEVIN MAYHEW LTD
Buxhall, Stowmarket, Suffolk, IP14 3BW
E-mail: info@kevinmayhewltd.com
Website: www.kevinmayhew.com

9 8 7 6 5 4 3 2 1 0

ISBN 978 1 84867 023 5
Catalogue No. 1501103

Design by Chris Coe
Edited by Katherine Laidler
Illustrations by Melody-Anne Lee & Steve English

Printed and bound in the EU

Contents

Introduction

When it is dark, we put on a light or light a candle; we do not struggle in the darkness but seek light. Once there was a little boy who attended a nativity concert. His parents were not there and people were worried about him walking home on his own on a dark road. When asked if he was afraid, he constantly and firmly said 'No'. When the concert was over, he produced a large torch and said, 'I am not afraid because I have this light.' The light gave him courage. Then, with a big smile, he said, 'And my father is waiting for me outside.' There was no need to be afraid because he had not only light but also someone who cared for him and loved him to go with him.

When we pray, we turn to our God who loves us and cares for us. In turning to him we turn away from darkness and turn not only to light but to our God who is always ready to help us. God wants us to share with him all that we do. He will not make us pray or force his presence on to us. He waits until we turn to him and invite him to be our friend. God's presence in our lives gives us courage and strength.

These prayers are to help you know that God loves you and is with you. Use the same prayer for a few days until you know it off by heart, then move on to another prayer. By learning prayers as you speak to God, it helps you to realise that God is with you and cares for you always. It is a good idea to make a special time and place each day to say your prayers. It is like when you meet with a friend; if you do not fix a place and time, you may not meet up. Spend some time in silence, just knowing that God is with you and that he loves you, and then use a prayer and let the prayer encourage you to pray words of your own.

By praying we learn to walk in the light and love of the Lord - may God help you to do this.

David Adam

Christmas Prayers

Jesus, I am getting ready
to celebrate your birthday.
Let me make sure I make room for you that day.
As you come to me in love,
may I come to you
and give you my love.
Amen.

God, thank you for Joseph
and that he cared for Mary.
I am glad he did what you asked him to do.
Help me to do what you want me to do.
Amen.

Father, thank you
that Jesus was born in the city of David
and that he came to be our Saviour.
As the shepherds came to see the baby Jesus
may I rejoice in his birth.
Amen.

God, thank you that you sent Jesus
to be our Saviour,
to heal the ill
and to bring joy to the world.
I pray that I may be ready to celebrate
his coming into the world.
Amen.

Lord Jesus, thank you
for the wise men and their gifts.
I love you as my King, my God
and my Saviour.
Amen.

God, thank you
for the escape of Jesus into Egypt.
I pray for all refugees
and those whose lives are in danger at this time.
Amen.

God, thank you for my parents,
for all the love and care they give me,
and thank you for the love and care
that Mary and Joseph gave to the baby Jesus.
Amen.

Lord Jesus, thank you
for coming to live among us.
You come to share in our lives
and to give us your love.
May I give my love to you
and know that you are with me.
Amen.

GOD, WE THANK
YOU FOR A
VERY SPECIAL
PRESENT,
JESUS

Easter Prayers

Lord Jesus, risen from the dead,
I believe in you,
I trust in you,
I love you.
You are my Lord and my God.
Amen.

Lord Jesus, I rejoice today in your resurrection.
I am pleased that you appeared
to Mary Magdalene
and you showed her that you were alive.
May I trust in you as my risen Lord,
for you are always with me and ready to help me.
Amen.

Father, thank you for Jesus
and that he offered his life for us.
He died on the cross for us all
and rose again
that we might share in life eternal.
Thank you for Jesus.
Amen.

Jesus, I am so happy
that you rose again from the dead.
You are alive and with me wherever I go.
Help me to keep in contact with you
through my prayers
and so know that you are my friend and Saviour.
Amen.

God our Father, thank you
for the resurrection of Jesus,
that he is alive and is my friend.
Jesus, I know that you are alive
and I am happy to say,
'Jesus is risen. Alleluia.'
Amen.

Lord Jesus, risen from the dead,
help me to know you are alive,
you are with me
and you love me.
Through my prayers
may I make you one of my friends
and know that you are with me to help me.
Amen.

God,
thank you that seeds and bulbs grow in secret
without me seeing them.
I trust they will rise out of the earth.
Thank you for Jesus who,
though crucified, dead and buried,
rose again for us all.
Amen.

Lord Jesus, you are unseen yet always near.
I believe in you.
I trust you.
I love you.
Help me to tell others of you
and of your resurrection.
Amen.

God's beautiful world

Lord God, thank you for the world
and all that is in it.
Teach me to care for it
and for all your creatures.
Let me not be responsible for the hurt
or spoiling of anything,
but let me help to make your world
a good place to live in.
Amen.

God, thank you for this wonderful world
and for our marvellous lives.
Help me to help keep your world clean
and free from evil,
and to enjoy living and working for you.
Amen.

God, thank you for the sounds of birds
and that I am able to hear.
Help me to listen carefully
and to be quiet in my prayers.
Amen.

Lord God, all power and strength belongs to you
for you have created the heavens and the earth
and all that is in them.
May I give my love to you each day
and care for the world that you have given us.
Amen.

God, you made the world and all that is in it.
You sent your Son Jesus Christ
to show your love and to be our Saviour.
Help me to be careful and respectful
in how I use your world
and to give thanks and worship you.
Amen.

God, you have chosen to make this wonderful world
and to give us life.
As you love me and give me so many things,
help me to show my love to you
by doing what you want me to do.
Amen.

God, you have made all things
out of your love and for your love.
Help me to show my love to you
in the way I care for the world.
Amen.

For the world in which I live
thank you, God.
For all I am able to do
thank you, God.
For all who provide me with food
thank you, God.
For all who love me
thank you, God.
For your love and generosity
thank you, God.
Amen.

God, help me to love the world
the way you do.
Teach me to respect all creatures
and not to make any suffer
through my greed or neglect.
May I know at all times
that you love me.
Amen.

God, thank you for our good
and beautiful world.
You have made all things for us to enjoy
and to care for.
May I always do what you want me to do
and be kind and good to others.
Amen.

God, thank you for life and health.
Thank you for the world in which we live
and for all my loved ones.
Each day may I give you thanks and praise
for all that you have done for me.
Amen.

God, thank you for a wonderful
and beautiful world.
Thank you for the love and care of my parents.
Help me to care for the world
and make sure that I do not spoil it for others.
Amen.

God's wonderful love

God, you made us out of your love
and you want us to love you.
I give my love to you this day.
Help me to show your love to others
by the way I deal with each of them.
Amen.

God, I know that you love me
and wait for me to turn to you.
You are always ready to hear me and help me.
Let me remember you
and your power every day.
Amen.

God, you are all-powerful
and a generous God,
always ready to help us
and give us of your goodness.
Thank you for my life and all I am able to do.
Amen.

Lord God, I am loved by you
and seek to love you.
You love all your creation –
help me to love it too.
Teach me to love others
as I know I am loved.
And thank you for all who love me.
Amen.

Lord God, you are wonderful,
greater than all treasures.
I am happy to know you love me
and are with me.
Help me to do what you would like me to do.
Amen.

Lord our God, you are the only God
and I love you with all my heart,
with all my mind and with all my strength
today and every day.
Amen.

God, you love me
and want me to spend time with you.
In the stillness you offer me your peace,
your power and your presence.
Help me to be still and quiet before you.
Amen.

God, I thank you for your love
and that you are always with me.
Jesus, help me to know you are always with me
and that I can talk to you about all I am doing.
I know you want to keep me safe
and in your peace.
Amen.

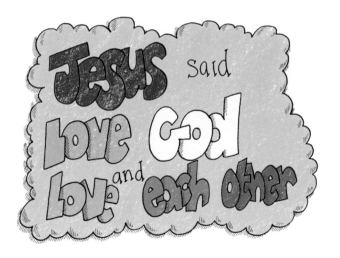

God, teach me to be still and quiet before you,
so that I may know your love for me
and give my love to you.
In the stillness help me to know
you are always with me
and that you care for every one of us.
Amen.

Thank you, God, for inviting me
to know you and love you.
I seek to enjoy your presence
and the wonderful world you have given us.
Amen.

God is always with us

God, you were there at the beginning
of the world
and the beginning of life.
Thank you that you are always with me.
You never leave me.
You are always ready to help me.
Amen.

Lord God, you care for me and love me.
You never leave me but are always there,
ready to help me and give me strength.
Help me to love you
and put my trust in you each day.
Amen.

Lord God,
I often do not know where I am going
or what will happen next,
but I know that you are always with me
and you love me.
Thank you, God.
Amen.

Lord Jesus, you are with me,
always with me.
Though you are hidden,
help me to know you are always there
and ready to be my friend.
Amen.

Christ before me.
Christ on my right.
Christ behind me.
Christ on my left.
Christ beneath me.
Christ above me.
Christ in my heart.
Christ in all who love me.

As the clouds hide the sun,
so you are hidden from me, O God.
Let me know that you are always there,
you are always with me.
You love me and never leave me.
Amen.

God, thank you that wherever I go
you are there.
You never leave me
and are always ready to help me and hear me.
Amen.

God, thank you
that you have many hidden surprises in life
and in my own life.
I trust in you
and I believe that you will keep me safe
for ever.
Amen.

Jesus is the Light of the World

Jesus, you are the Light of the World.
When we know you,
you bring brightness and hope to our lives.
I know that you are God's Son
and I love you.
Amen.

Lord Jesus, help me to walk in your light
so that I may reflect your love
and so bring others to you
and to the brightness and life
that you offer to all.
Amen.

Lord Jesus, it is wonderful to know you.
You are my friend and you are the Light
that chases away the darkness of our world.
Help me to love you every day.
Amen.

God our Father, thank you for Jesus
who is the Light of the World.
Thank you that he shows your love for us.
May we learn to love you more and more
every day.
Amen.

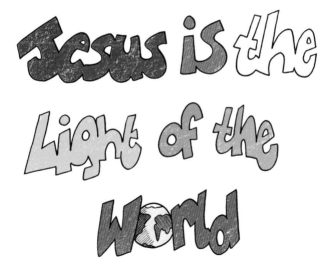

Jesus is King

Jesus, you are the King of kings.
You are the ruler of the whole world.
Yet in love you come to serve us and help us.
You gave your life for us.
Help me to give myself to you
and to serve you by caring for others.
Amen.

Jesus, you are the Servant King.
Help me to care for others
and spend time looking after them.
Amen.

Jesus, you are my King and my God.
I want to love you and serve you always.
Help me to do your will
and so be part of your kingdom.
Amen.

Jesus, we welcome you with joy
and with shouts of Hosanna
for you are our King and the Prince of Peace.
Through you, may we have peace
in our hearts, in our homes and in the world.
Amen.

Jesus, my King and my God,
let me work for you,
let me tell of you,
let me love you,
let me obey you
and let me be part of your kingdom.
Amen.

Jesus, I welcome you as my King.
Come rule in my heart.
I know that you love me
and you are my Saviour.
Come, Lord Jesus, as King
and help me.
Amen.

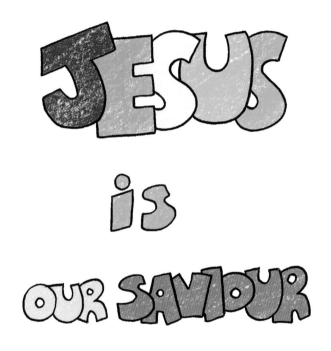

Jesus is great!

Lord Jesus, you came
that we should enjoy living
and to give us life that is eternal.
Thank you for your power and presence
with us always.
Amen.

Lord Jesus, you are the Good Shepherd.
You seek out the troubled and the lost
to bring them safely home.
Teach me always to be generous
and to care for others as you care for me.
Amen.

Jesus, you look after me
as a shepherd would look after his sheep.
I thank you for your love and care
and ask you to protect me in all dangers.
Amen.

Come, Jesus,
be known as my companion and friend.
Let me know that you are ever with me
and love me
and help me to work for you.
Amen.

Lord Jesus, you are the Prince of Peace.
You stilled the waves, the storm
and the troubled mind of the madman.
Let me live in your peace
and know your power in my life.
Amen.

Thank you, God, for water,
for rain, rivers and seas,
for wells, reservoirs and tap water.
Thank you for Jesus, the Water of Life.
Amen.

Jesus, help me to know you as my friend
and as my Saviour and my God.
Thank you for all the wonderful things you do.
Help me to know your power and your love.
Amen.

Lord Jesus,
thank you for all that you have done for me
and that you love me always.
Amen.

Father, Son
and Holy Spirit

Father, thank you for the creation of the world
and for giving us life.
Jesus, thank you for living and dying for us,
that we may share in life eternal.
Spirit, thank you for your power
and that you are always ready to guide us.
I give my love to you,
Father, Son and Holy Spirit.
Amen.

Father, you are my Creator.
Jesus, you are my Saviour.
Spirit, you are my Guide.
Thank you for your love
and your presence with me
today and always.
Amen.

Father God, I love you
and I know you love me.
Jesus, Son of God, I love you
and I know you love me.
Spirit of God, I love you
and I know you love me.
May I do the work that you want me to do always.
Amen.

Father, thank you for the world and for loving me.
I give my love to you.
Jesus, thank you for loving me,
for dying and rising again.
I give my love to you.
Spirit, thank you for loving me,
for helping me and guiding me.
I give my love to you.
Amen.

Friends of Jesus

Lord Jesus, as the fishermen listened to you
and followed you,
help me to follow you each day
and be part of your team.
Let me show my love for you
and do what you would like me to do.
Amen.

Lord Jesus, I would like to be on your team
to fight against evil and to do good.
Help me to be your friend
and to work for you and your kingdom.
Let me not give in to evil but seek to help you.
Amen.

Jesus, help me to listen to your word
and seek to do your will.
May I show that I love you
by doing what you want me to do.
Amen.

Jesus, you are wonderful.
Help me to tell others of your love
and your saving power.
Show me how to share with my friends
the Good News that I have learnt.
Amen.

Lord Jesus, as you gave your life for me
and offer me your friendship,
help me to be your close friend
and to talk with you each day.
May I give my love and my life
to work for you and your glory.
Amen.

Jesus, I love you
and want to shine as a light in your world.
Help me to show I love you
by saying my prayers
and by telling others about you.
Amen.

Lord Jesus,
help me to know that in obeying you
my life is enriched and changed
into something precious and wonderful.
Amen.

Lord Jesus, help me to fight against evil.
Deliver me from temptation
and make me strong to serve you.
Amen.

Take my hands, Lord Jesus,
let them work for you.
Let me share in helping
and in caring for others.
Let my hands show your love,
Jesus, Friend and Healer.
Amen.

Lord Jesus,
as the fishermen listened to you
and obeyed you,
help me to be ready to do
what you want me to do.
Amen.

Prayers in times of trouble

God, you are strong and loving.
I am always in your hands.
You hold on to me even when I am in trouble
and you still love me.
You help me to begin again and to do new things.
Thank you, God.
Amen.

Lord, may I come to you in the stillness
and trust in you in the storms.
Help me to know you are always with me
and ready to offer me your helping hand.
Amen.

Lord Jesus, your hands are full of power.
You heal and you bring comfort to people.
When I am troubled
let me learn to put my hand in yours
and to trust in you.
Amen.

Lord God, you are always with me,
even when times are bad.
You never stop loving me
and you are always ready to help me.
At all times let me remember you
and your love.
Amen.

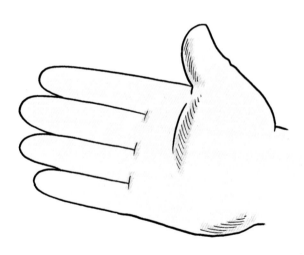

Lord Jesus, when I am in trouble
you are close by.
You, Lord, are my Saviour and are
ready to help me.
I give thanks for your presence
and rest in your power and peace,
Jesus Christ my Lord and Saviour.
Amen.

Holy and strong God,
protect me from all that is evil.
Keep me in your presence,
surround me with your power
and keep me in your peace.
Amen.

God, thank you for your love and protection.
Whatever happens in this world,
you still love me and care for me.
Help me to know your power
and to be aware of your presence.
Amen.

God, you are always with me.
You keep me in your love
and you protect me from evil.
Help me to remember that you never leave me
and you are always happy to hear my prayers.
Amen.

Prayers when
I am sorry

God, thank you that you love me always.
When I am sorry
you forgive me what I have done wrong
and you welcome me with love.
God, help me to do
what you would like me to do
and to be the person you would like me to be.
Amen.

God, thank you that you always love me.
When I do wrong you do not like what I do
but you still love me.
Help me to say sorry when I do wrong
and to give my love to you.
Amen.

God, I want to give my whole life to you.
I am sorry for when I have done wrong
and ask you to forgive me.
I will try to live a good life
and to do what you would have me do,
so that your kingdom may come on earth
as it is in heaven.
Amen.

God, you have made me for a good purpose
and to be useful to you and to others.
When I fail to do what you want
forgive me and help me to start again.
Amen.

Father, thank you for your love for me
and for giving me life.
Thank you for all who love me
and care for me
even when I do wrong.
Help me to be loving and caring
and to forgive from my heart
those who have upset or hurt me.
Amen.

God, you love me always.
Even when I have done things
that make you sad
you still love me and always love me.
Thank you, God.
Amen.

Prayers for other people

God, there are lots of hungry and poor people
in our world.
Show me how to help them
and not to be greedy with what I have.
Let me learn to share and to care
as you care for me.
Amen.

Jesus, thank you for your love
towards all people.
I pray to you for all who are ill or troubled
at this time.
May they know you are with them
and want to help them always.
Amen.

God, thank you for the bravery
of all who work in the rescue services.
Thank you that Jesus came
to rescue us from death
and to bring us to eternal life.
Amen.

Lord Jesus, you love everyone
and are concerned when anyone suffers.
Help me to care for all who are
in need or in trouble.
Amen.

God, thank you for my eyes.
I am grateful that I can see,
I can read,
I can enjoy colour and light.
I pray for all who suffer from blindness
or whose lives are darkened by poor sight.
Amen.

Jesus, I know that you love me
and care for me.
I pray for all the hungry people in the world.
Show me how I can help them
to know of your love and care.
Amen.

Jesus, thank you for your love
and your power to heal.
I ask your blessing
upon all who are ill or suffering
at this time.
Amen.

Lord Jesus, thank you for healing people
and making them well.
Help me to keep in touch with you
through my prayers.
Amen.

Also available:

Sharing the light
1501102

The best way to show your child that you believe in God
is to talk to God in their presence and to encourage
them to talk to God in their own simple words.

The prayers in this book are to assist your own prayers
and your child's. Spend a little time together each day
simply rejoicing in the presence and turning to the light
and love of God. Say the prayers together so that they
are not simply recited but learnt by heart – that is,
learnt by worship and not by the mind alone.

Prayer is a great adventure and the opening of
our lives to the love and light of our God.
Enjoy that adventure with your child.

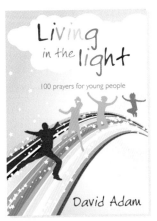

Living in the light
1501104

God – Father, Son and Holy Spirit – seeks to be our friend. But we can only truly be friends if we spend time with each other, talk to each other and express our love for each other. We can do this by setting aside some time each day to remind ourselves of the love and presence of God. The more we become aware of God and his love, the more we are able to be fully alive. It is like coming out of darkness and living in the light.

These prayers are to help you in this adventure. They are not to replace your own words but rather to help you see how great God is and how to speak to him. Use the words to make you aware of the reality behind them: God is with you and God loves you.